Early Music For Rec

MW00785267

Amsco Publications
London/New York/Sydney

Exclusive Distributors:
Music Sales Limited
8/9 Frith Street, London W1V 5TZ
Music Sales Corporation
257 Park Avenue South, New York, NY 10016, USA
Music Sales Pty. Limited
120 Rothschild Avenue, Rosebery, NSW 2018, Australia

This book © Copyright 1984 by
Amsco Publications
ISBN 0.7119.0499.5
Order No. AM 36542

All songs © Copyright 1984 Dorsey Brothers Music Ltd., 8/9 Frith Street, London W1V 5TZ

Designed by Howard Brown
Cover photography by Peter Wood
Arranged and compiled by Robin De Smet

Music Sales complete catalogue lists thousands of titles and is free from your local music book shop,
or direct from Music Sales Limited.
Please send a cheque or postal order for £1.50 for postage to Music Sales Limited, 8/9 Frith Street, London W1V 5TZ.

Printed in England by
Halstan & Co. Limited, Amersham, Bucks.

Douce Dame Jolie

Guillaume de Machaut

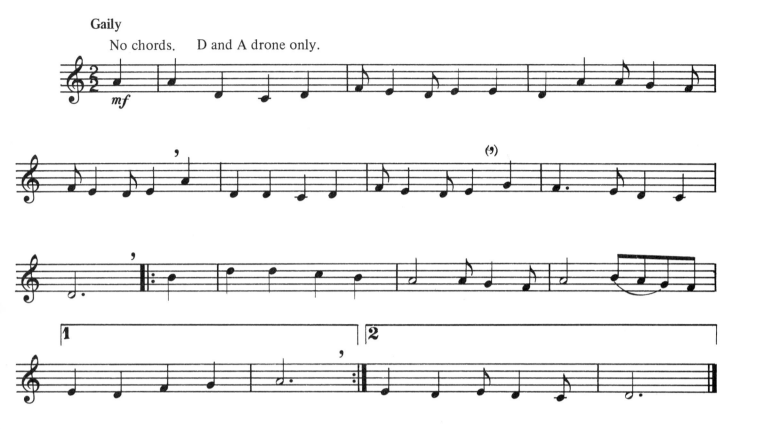

Gaily

No chords. D and A drone only.

The Earl of Salisbury's Pavan

William Byrd

Moderato

The Carman's Whistle

William Byrd

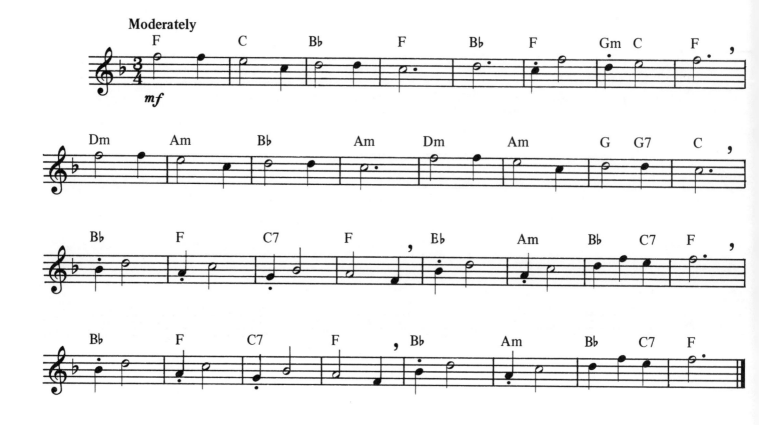

Courante

Johann Schop

Blow Thy Horn Hunter

William Cornysh

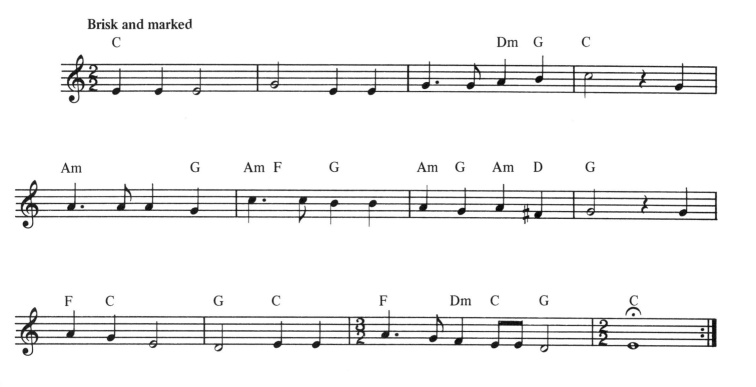

Branle De L'Official

Anon. 16th Century

Branle No. 1

Claude Gervaise

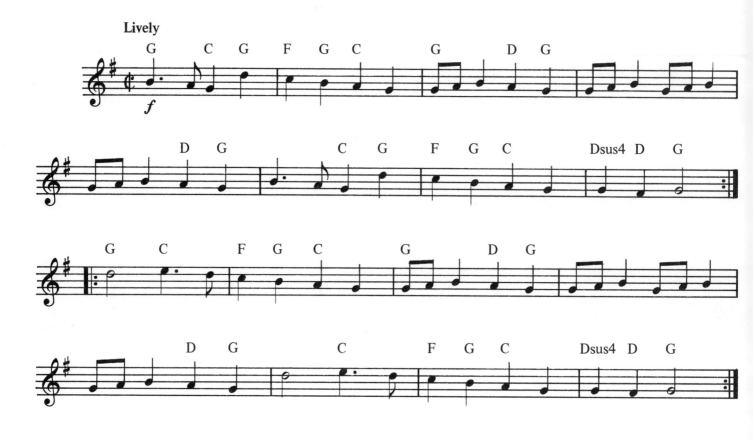

Branle No. 2

Claude Gervaise

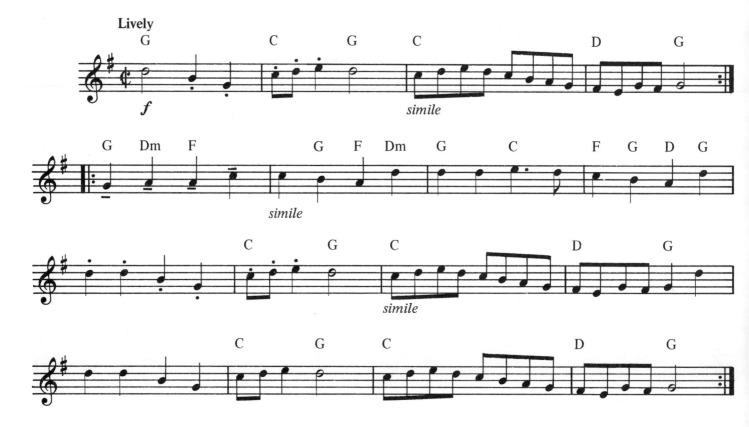

All In The Garden Green

Anon. 16th Century

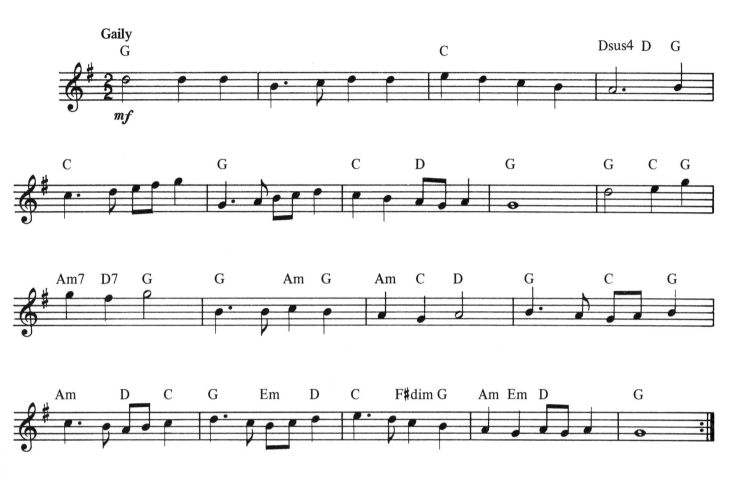

Belle Qui Tiens Ma Vie

Anon. 16th Century

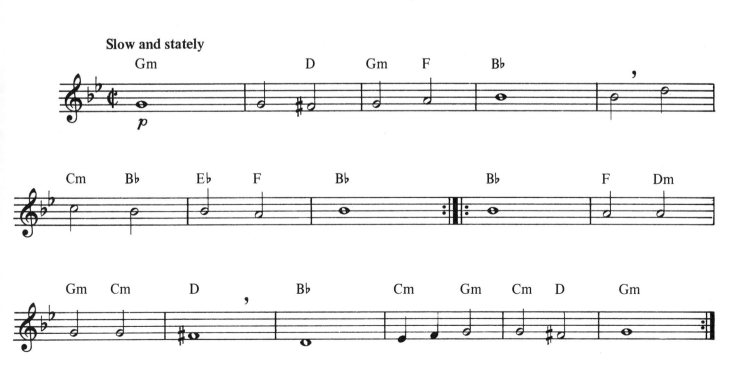

Fortune My Foe

Anon. 16th Century

Greensleeves

Anon. 16th Century

How Should I Your True Love Know?

Traditional

The Honie-Suckle

Anthony Holborne

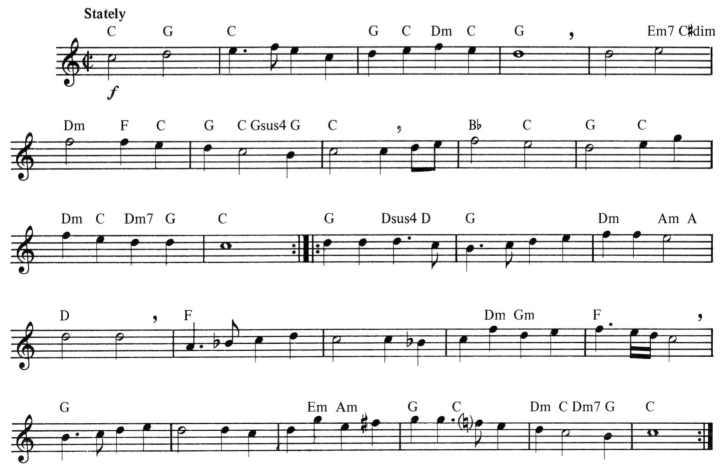

If My Complaints

John Dowland

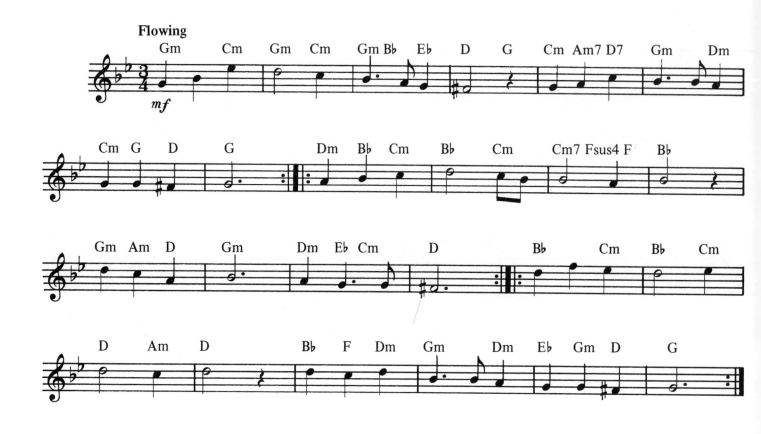

The King Of Denmark Galliard

John Dowland

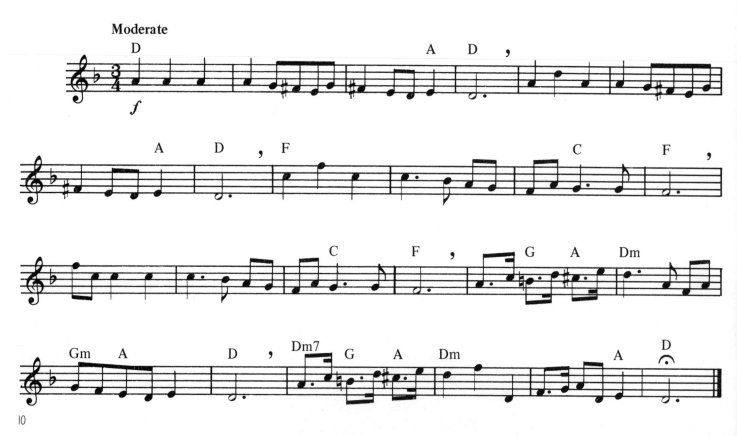

Never Weather-Beaten Sail

Thomas Campion

Now Is The Month Of Maying

Thomas Morley

Minuet

Louis Couperin

Minuet

Henry Purcell

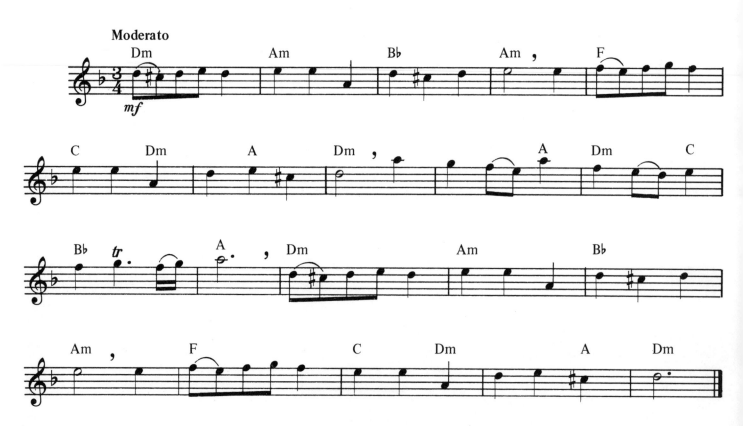

Pastime With Good Company

Henry VIII

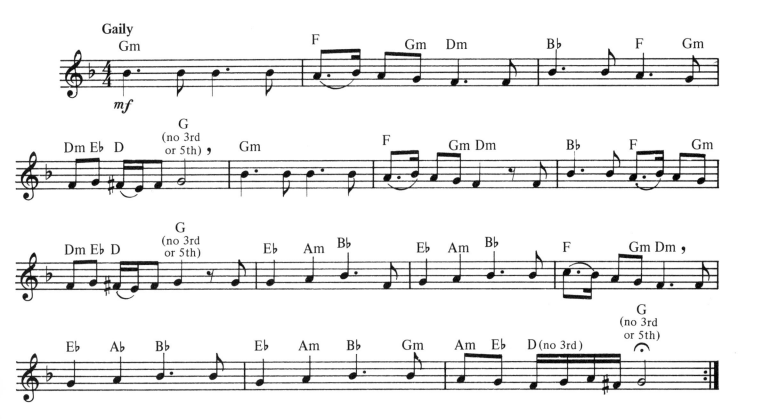

Parson's Farewell

Traditional

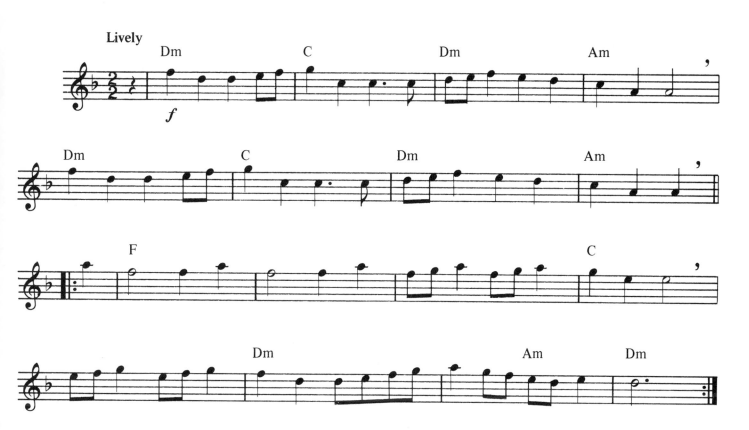

Now, Oh Now My Needs Must Part

John Dowland

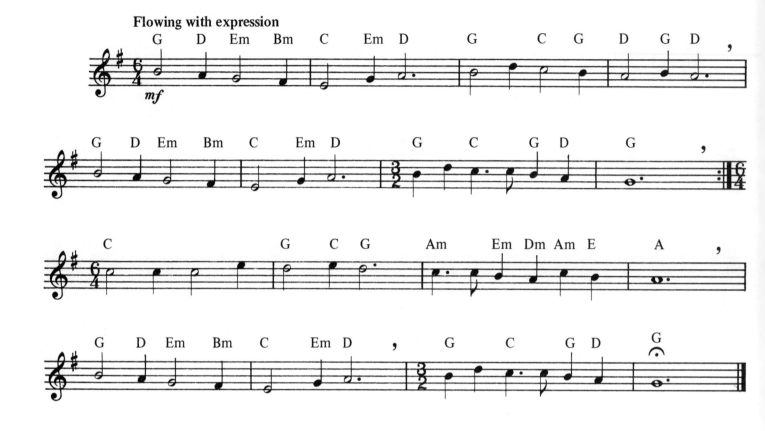

The Oil Of Barley

Traditional

Quant Je Suis Mis

Guillaume de Machaut

Moderate and tenderly

No chords

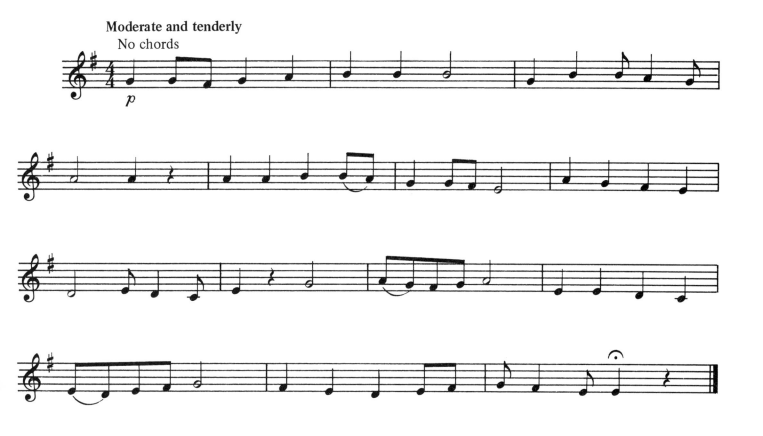

The Sick Tune

Anon. 16th Century

Slow

The Silver Swan

Orlando Gibbons

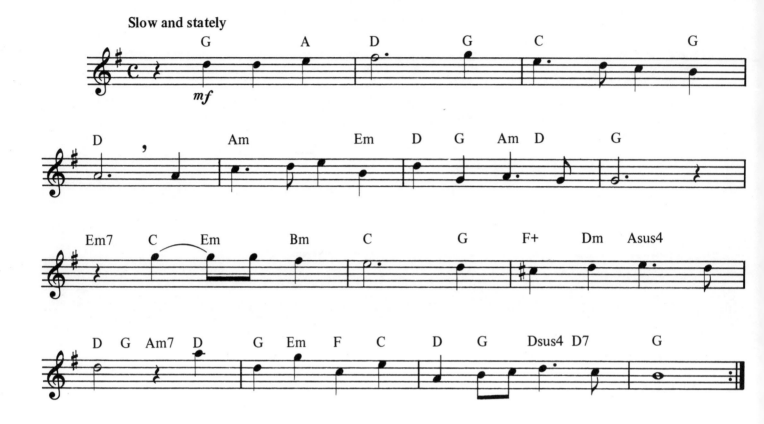

Tourdion

Anon. 16th Century

When Phoebus First Did Daphne Love

John Dowland

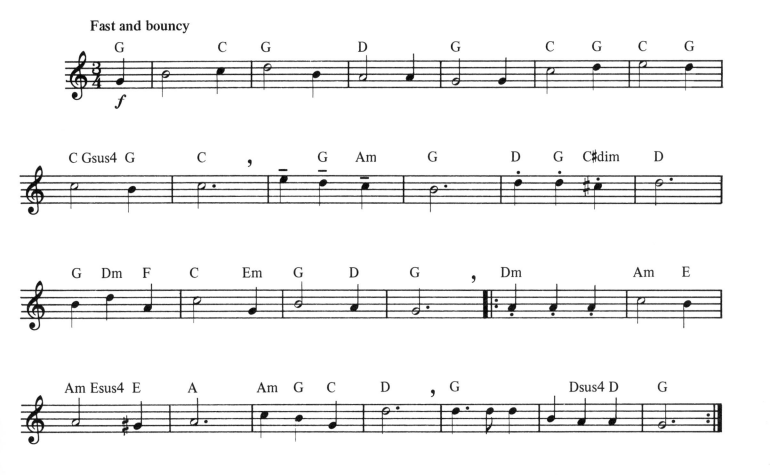

When That I Was And A Little Tiny Boy

Anon. 16th Century

The Willow Song

Anon. 16th Century

Winder Wie Ist

Neithart Von Reuenthal

Summer Is Icumen In

Anon. 13th Century

A Round In Four Parts

Danse Royale

Anon. 13th Century

Branle De Bourgogne

Claude Gervaise

Edi Beo
(Duet)
Anon. 13th Century

Minuet

Jean Henri D'Anglebert

O Admirabile Veneris Ydolum

Anon. 10th or 11th Century

Tristan's Lament

Anon. 14th Century

Ronde

Tielman Susato

Narrenaufzug

Tielman Susato

Move Now With Measured Sound

Thomas Campion

Saltarello

Anon. 14th Century

Green Groweth The Holly

Henry VIII (Attrib.)

Matona Mia Cara

Orlando Di Lasso

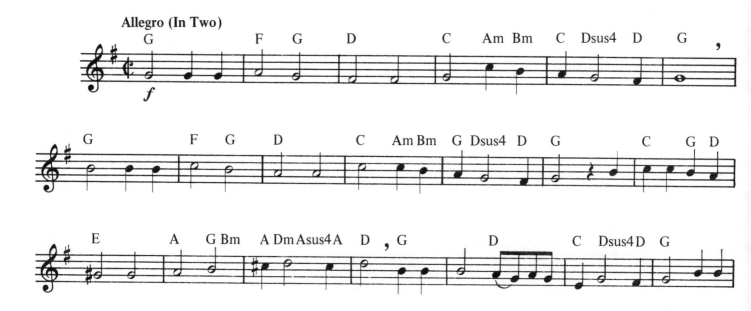

rall.....   en - tando

Bergamasca

Anon. 16th Century

Blame Not My Lute

Anon. 16th Century

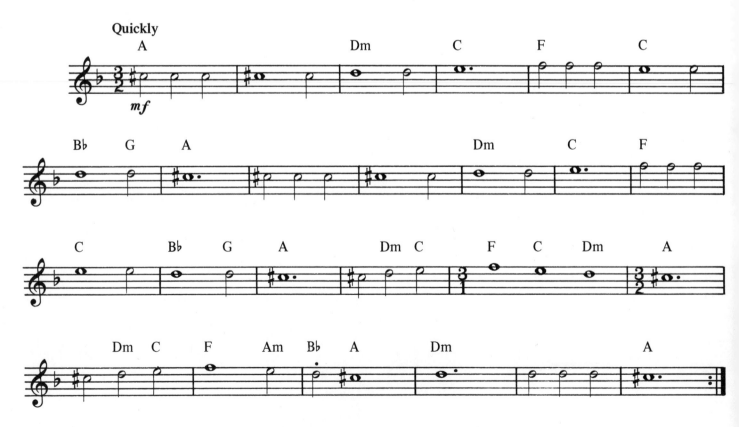

3/94 (17515)